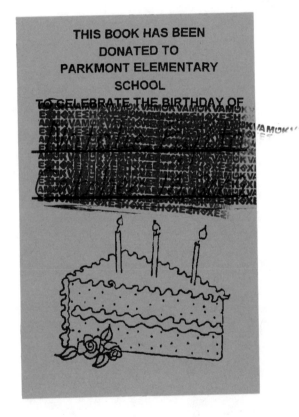

**THIS BOOK HAS BEEN
DONATED TO
PARKMONT ELEMENTARY
SCHOOL
TO CELEBRATE THE BIRTHDAY OF**

TAKING SIDES

Exploring Geometry

Nancy Harris

Rourke
Publishing LLC

Vero Beach, Florida 32964

www.rourkepublishing.com

PHOTO CREDITS: title page ©

Editor: Robert Stengard-Olliges

Cover design by Nicola Stratford, bdpublishing.com

Library of Congress Cataloging-in-Publication Data

Harris, Nancy.
  Taking sides : exploring geometry / Nancy Harris.
      p. cm. -- (Math focal points)
  Includes index.
  ISBN 978-1-60044-644-3
  1. Geometry--Juvenile literature. I. Title. II. Series.

  QA445.5.H373 2008
  516--dc22

                          2007018046

Printed in the USA

CG/CG

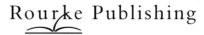

www.rourkepublishing.com – rourke@rourkepublishing.com
Post Office Box 3328, Vero Beach, FL 32964

Table of Contents

Taking Sides

Cassidy and Ainsley had to share a bedroom. Their room had four equal **sides** and four right **angles**. How would they share their square room?

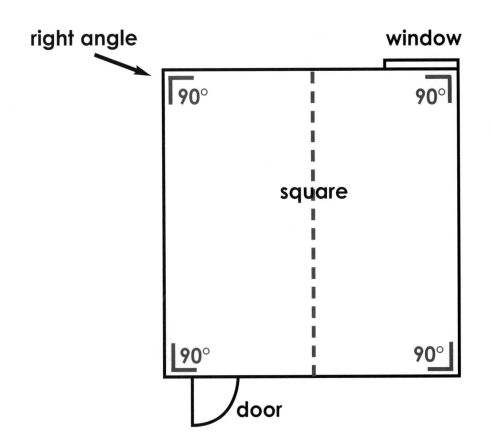

The two girls decided to **divide** the room in half. They put a **line** down the middle of the room.

Each half of the room had two long sides, two short sides, and four right angles. The girls had two rectangle shaped spaces now.

Cassidy picked the side by the window. Ainsley got the side by the door.

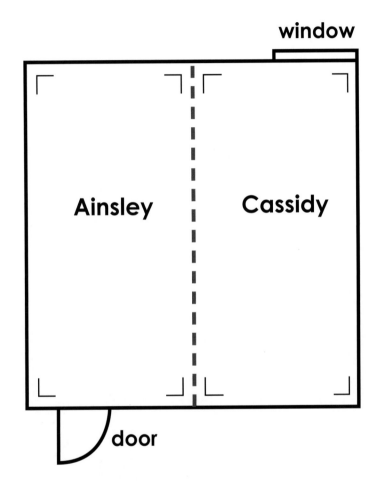

window

Ainsley   Cassidy

door

7

Beds

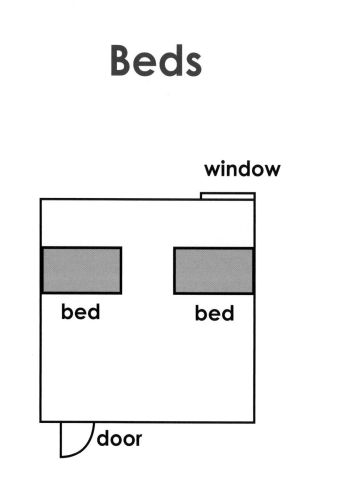

First, the girls tried putting the beds in the two top corners of the room. Hmmm... This left a big open space in the middle.

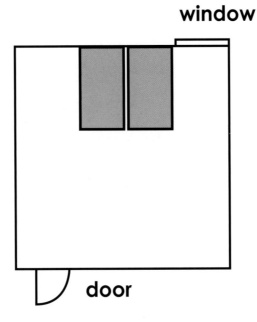

door

They decided to try pushing the beds together in the middle of the room. What shape is the big bed? Why?

Dresser

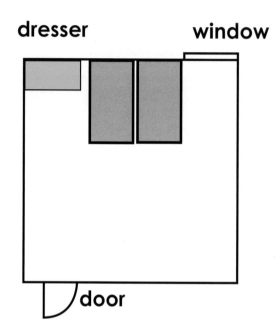

dresser   window

door

Next, the girls slid the dresser into the back left corner of the room.

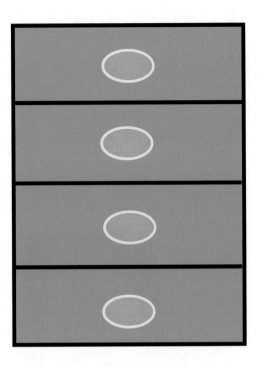

The dresser had four rectangle drawers with oval handles. Each girl claimed two dresser drawers.

Desks and End Tables

Cassidy suggested that they bring in the two tables they used for desks. Each table top had one long side, two short sides, and three angles. The tables were triangle shaped.

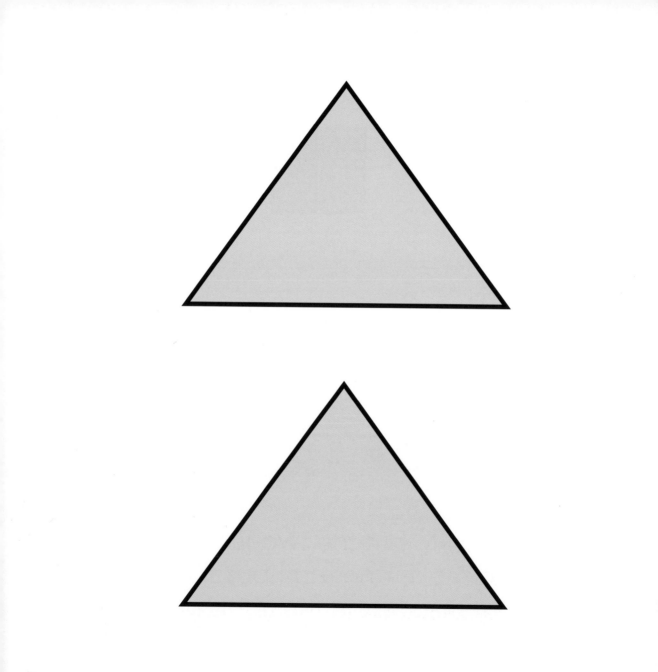

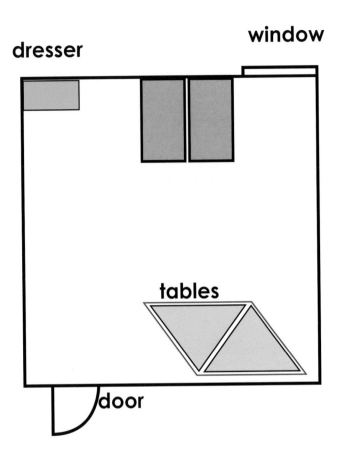

They decided to put the two triangle tables together to make one rhombus shaped desk. The girls put the desk in the right hand corner of the room.

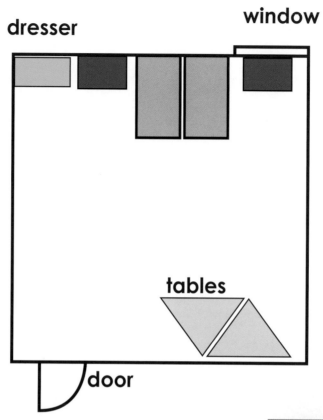

dresser

window

tables

door

Now, Ainsley brought in the end tables. These two tables had drawers with circle handles. They would work on either side of their big bed.

15

Lamps

There was a light in the center of the ceiling but they needed more light by their bed and desk. Their dad gave them two small lamps for their end tables. The girls saw many different shapes in the lamps. What shapes do you see?

When you looked at the sides of the lampshades, two of the four sides were **parallel** to each other. The shape was a trapezoid.

For the desk they found the perfect lamp. It had a metal shade that the girls could move. What shape is the lamp?

Bedding and Mirrors

Now came the fun part. The girls went shopping with their mom to buy a new bedspread. What colors and shapes can you see on the bedspread and wall?

They also bought some fun mirrors to hang on the walls. What shapes are the mirrors? How do you know?

One Side

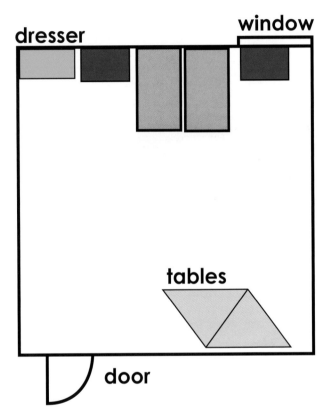

The girls realized their new room no longer had two rectangle sides. Instead it was just one large square again. They didn't mind having only one side to the room. It was their side, their bed, and their room.

Glossary

angle (ANG uhl) — an angle is where two lines meet

oval (OH vuhl) — a shape like an egg

parallel (PAR ruh lel) — two straight lines that are the same distance apart

rectangle (REK tang guhl) — a shape with two long sides, two short sides, and four right angles

rhombus (ROM buhss) — a shape that has four straight sides of equal length but usually does not have right angles

side (SIDE) — a line on the edge of an object

square (SKWAIR) — a line on the edge of an object

trapezoid (TRAP uh zoid) — a shape with four sides of which only two are parallel

triangle (TRYE an guhl) — a closed shape with three straight sides and three angles

Index

Further Reading

James, Christianne. *Party of Three: A Book About Triangles*. Picture Window Books, 2006.

Martin, Elena. *So Many Circles*. Yellow Umbrella Books, 2006.

Shepard, Daniel. *Solid Shapes*. Yellow Umbrella Books, 2006.

Recommended Websites

www.funbrain.com/poly

www.arcytech.org/java/patterns

www.mathplayground.com

About the Author

Nancy Harris is an educational consultant with twenty years teaching experience. She enjoys writing nonfiction books and teaching students and educators nonfiction reading strategies. She currently lives in Lafayette, Colorado.